Ellen Ochoa

by Michelle Parkin

NORWOOD HOUSE PRESS

Cover: Ellen Ochoa is a leader in space science.

Norwood House Press
For information regarding Norwood House Press, please visit our website at:
www.norwoodhousepress.com or call 866-565-2900.

Hardcover ISBN: 978-1-68450-745-0
Paperback ISBN: 978-1-68404-821-2

Library of Congress Cataloging-in-Publication Data

Names: Parkin, Michelle, 1984- author.
Title: Ellen Ochoa / by Michelle Parkin.
Description: [Chicago] : Norwood House Press, [2023] | Series: STEM superstars | Includes index. | Audience: Ages 5-8 | Audience: Grades K-1 | Summary: "Describes the life and work of Ellen Ochoa, the first Hispanic woman to become a NASA astronaut and the former director of the Johnson Space Center"-- Provided by publisher.
Identifiers: LCCN 2022037332 (print) | LCCN 2022037333 (ebook) | ISBN 9781684507450 (hardcover) | ISBN 9781684048212 (paperback) | ISBN 9781684048410 (epub)
Subjects: LCSH: Ochoa, Ellen--Juvenile literature. | Women astronauts--United States--Biography--Juvenile literature. | Hispanic American astronauts--United States--Biography--Juvenile literature. | Hispanic American women--Biography--Juvenile literature.
Classification: LCC TL789.85.O25 P37 2023 (print) | LCC TL789.85.O25 (ebook) | DDC 629.450092 [B]--dc23/eng/20221004
LC record available at https://lccn.loc.gov/2022037332
LC ebook record available at https://lccn.loc.gov/2022037333

359N–012023
Manufactured in the United States of America in North Mankato, Minnesota.

★ Table of Contents ★

Chapter 1

Early Life

Ellen Ochoa was born on May 10, 1958. She grew up in California. She has four brothers and sisters. When Ochoa was in middle school, her parents **divorced**. This was hard on her. Ochoa went to live with her mom.

Ochoa was born in Los Angeles, California.

Ochoa went on to play the flute in her college marching band.

Music was Ochoa's hobby. She played the flute. She learned when she was 10. Ochoa was a good student. She liked school. She was in the top of her class.

Did You Know?
Ochoa's love of math and science helped her become an astronaut.

Ochoa went to San Diego State University. She studied physics. At the time, few women had jobs in science. People said science classes would be too hard. Ochoa proved them wrong.

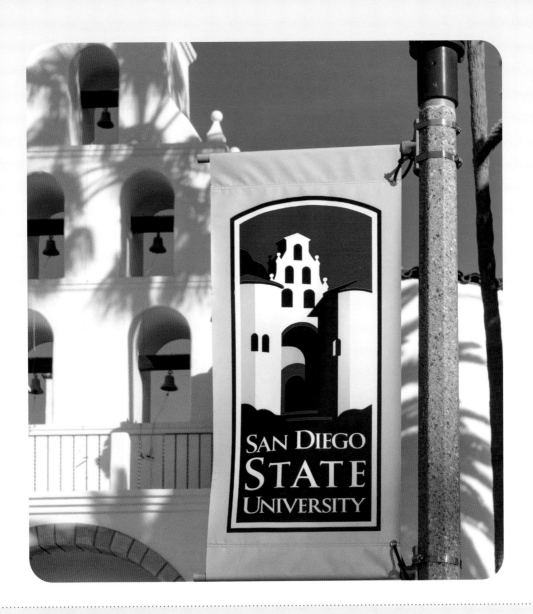

Sometimes, Ochoa was the only woman in her college classes.

Chapter 2

NASA Astronaut

Ochoa looked up to astronauts. Her **role models** were Sally Ride and Franklin Chang Diaz. Ochoa wanted to go to space too.

Sally Ride was the first American woman in space.

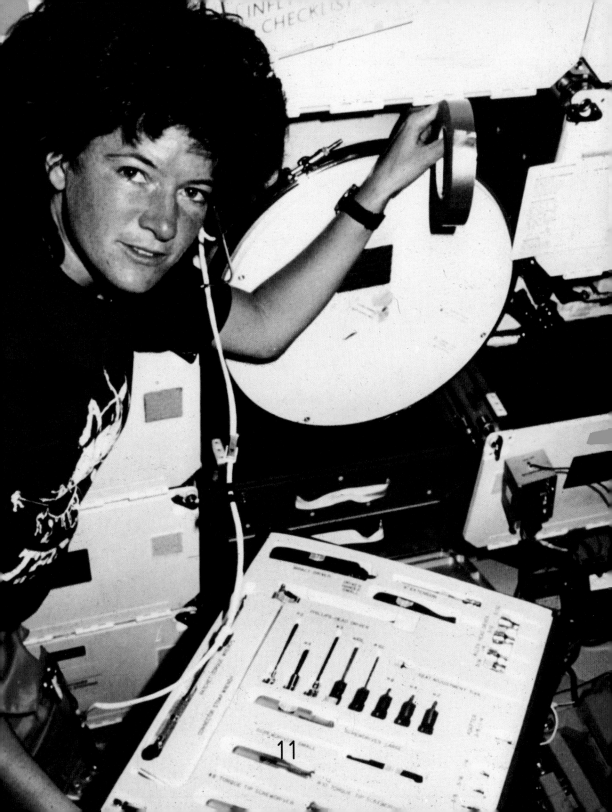

Ochoa applied to NASA. A lot of other people did too. Ochoa didn't get in the first time. She didn't give up. Finally, she got in. Ochoa started training. She became an astronaut.

Ochoa can also fly jet planes.

Ochoa has been on four space missions.

In 1993, Ochoa went on her first space mission. She was the first Hispanic female astronaut. She studied **energy** from the Sun. She saw how it affects Earth. Ochoa was in space for nine days.

Chapter 3

Back on Earth

In 2007, Ochoa stopped being an astronaut. She worked at Johnson Space Center. She became the **director**. Ochoa was the second woman to get this job.

Ochoa was the first Hispanic director for the space center.

The Orion can hold four people.

Ochoa worked on the Orion **spacecraft**. The Orion can take people farther into space than ever before.

Today, Ochoa talks to students about her trips to space. She wants to be a role model. She inspires kids who want to be astronauts too.

Ochoa worked hard to achieve her dreams.

SPACE CENTER
CENTER
21
HOUSTON

★ Career Connections ★

1. Ochoa studied physics in college. If you want to be an astronaut too, science and math are important. Think about joining a math or science club at school.

2. Ochoa played the flute since she was 10. Being a musician is hard work. It takes a lot of practice. To get started, talk to a parent about starting music lessons. Also, ask your music teacher about joining the school band.

3. Ochoa wanted to be an astronaut. She looked up to people who had that career. Go to the library. Read about someone with a career you like.

4. Ochoa was the first Hispanic female astronaut. Who are some other famous firsts? What could you be the first at in your future career?

5. Ochoa was an astronaut at NASA. You don't have to fly a spacecraft to explore the universe. Scientists, engineers, computer programmers, and others are doing important work at NASA too. Research what type of career you'd like to have there.

⭐ Glossary ⭐

director (duh-REK-tuhr): The person who guides a group of people or business.

divorced (di-VORST): Officially ended a marriage.

energy (EN-ur-jee): Power that produces heat.

NASA (NASS-uh): National Aeronautics and Space Administration, an American agency that works on air and space technology.

physics (FIZ-iks): The science that deals with matter and energy. It includes the study of light, heat, sound, electricity, motion, and force.

role models (ROHL MOD-uhlz): People others can look up to.

spacecraft (SPAYSS-kraft): A vehicle that travels or is used in space.

⭐ For More Information ⭐

Books

Mosca, Julia Finley. *The Astronaut with a Song for the Stars: The Story of Dr. Ellen Ochoa*. Amazing Scientists. Seattle, WA: The Innovation Press, 2019. Learn about Ellen Ochoa and her love of music and science.

Stoltman, Joan. *Ellen Ochoa*. Little Biographies of Big People. New York, NY: Gareth Stevens Publishing, 2019. Read this book to learn more about Ellen Ochoa and her life.

Websites

Ellen Ochoa
(www.ducksters.com/biography/explorers/ellen_ochoa.php) Learn fun facts about Ellen Ochoa.

NASA Kids' Club
(https://www.nasa.gov/kidsclub/index.html) Learn about space, planets, and more on this NASA website.

★ Index ★

★ About the Author ★

Michelle Parkin is an editor and a children's book author. She has written more than 15 children's books about famous people, animals, and dinosaurs. She lives with her daughter and golden retriever mix in Minnesota.